D0194974

This
Book
Belongs
To _

Grolier Enterprises Inc.
SHERMAN TURNPIKE, DANBURY, CONNECTICUT 06816

Book Club Edition

An
ALICE
IN
BIBLELAND ®
Storybook

The STORY Of DAVID And GOLIATH

Written by Alice Joyce Davidson
Illustrated by Victoria Marshall

Text copyright ©1985 by Alice Joyce Davidson
Art copyright ©1985 by The C.R. Gibson Company
Published by The C.R. Gibson Company
Norwalk, Connecticut 06856
Printed in the United States of America
All rights reserved
ISBN 0-8378-5070-3
D.L. TO: 2164-1988

A little girl named Alice
Liked to exercise and run
And to read a Bible story
When every day was done.

Alice liked to read about
How faith will see us through
And how everything is possible
When God is there with you.

Of young David and the giant
Was the story Alice read
When an airmail bird delivered
A little note which said:
"Reading is the magic key
That takes you where you want to be."

The Bible storybook she had
Became a great big screen.
Alice walked on through to Bibleland
And came upon this scene.

A shepherd boy named David
Could play the harp and sing.
David's older brothers
Were soldiers for the King.

David was too young to fight.
He watched his father's sheep,
Then sang and played the harp to help
King Saul of Israel sleep.

King Saul was very worried.
He couldn't sleep at night
Since the soldiers of the Philistines
Were looking for a fight.

Their champion was Goliath,
A giant almost ten feet tall.
And when he spoke, the Israelites
Would tremble one and all.

Goliath roared, "You Israelites,
Let's let our soldiers rest.
Just send one man to fight me
To decide which army's best.
And if your man can kill me
Here's what we will do.
We'll say you Israelites have won
And we'll be slaves for you."

"But if I win this battle
By being strong and clever,
You Israelites will work for us
And be our slaves forever!"

For forty days he challenged
The Israelites to fight.
They looked up at the giant
And their hearts were filled with fright.

One day young David brought some food
To help his brothers out.
He heard the great big giant
Named Goliath roar and shout.

David asked, "Why do you fear
Goliath's shouts and fuss?
We are all God's people;
He'll take good care of us."

David went before the King
And said to him, "King Saul,
I want to fight Goliath
Who is almost ten feet tall."
At first King Saul refused him.
"You are but a shepherd boy.
Goliath is a giant
Who can break you like a toy."

But David answered, "I have killed
A lion and a bear.
Each tried to take away some sheep
Grazing in my care."

"My strength and courage came from God.
He kept me safe back then,
And when I fight Goliath,
God will be with me again!"

At last King Saul said, "David, go;
God keep you in His care.
And for this brave deed that you do,
My armor's yours to wear."

But David didn't feel right
In the armor of the King,
Instead he picked up five smooth stones
And took his staff and sling.

Goliath looked at David
And gave a scornful laugh,
For he thought David couldn't win
With just a sling and staff.

Goliath said, "Come closer.
Come fight me if you dare,
And I will feed you to the beasts
And fowl that fill the air!"

Then David said, "You come to me
With armor, javelin and spear,
But I come in the name of God
And so I have no fear!
The Lord, my God, will conquer you.
He needs no spear or sword.
And everyone who follows Him
Will have a just reward!"

Goliath rushed at David.
His shield and weapons shone.
David took his sling out
And loaded one smooth stone.

David slung the little stone.
It hit Goliath's head.
It sunk into his forehead
And Goliath fell down dead.

The armies of the Philistines
Decided not to stay.
They knew that they had lost the war
So turned and ran away.